Advance Praise

"In this collection, Marianne Peel takes a reader on a journey of the heart—from Greece and Turkey to Nepal and China, from Ukraine to the US. With passion, curiosity, and a keen eye for detail, Peel introduces readers to places and lives that seem, on the surface, to be far removed from her own. These are people—loving, shattered, joy-filled, and oh so human—with whom Peel shares the intimacy of story, music, and dance. *No Distance Between Us* is indeed the message, not just for Peel in her travels, but for all of us who are transported with her."
—Laura Apol, author of *A Fine Yellow Dust*

"Marianne Peel's poems, inspired by travel around the world and refugee experience, reflect an astonishing awareness of detail, encompassing empathy and transformation. A haunting poetic accomplishment."
—Jan Freeman, author of *Blue Structure* and *Simon Says*

"Marianne Peel's evocative poetry collection travels to faraway places inside a rich diction. Her lyrical tenderness and compassion for humanity reveal a keen eye and an abundance of the heart. Each poem tells a story, and each story tells a truth. Stunning."
—Julie Maloney, founder and director of Women Reading Aloud

"As the Argentine writer Lucio Mansilla once ironically noted, 'we travel to broaden our minds, only to forget what little we have learned on this earth.' Yet, there are those who travel with awareness, who travel with one eye trained on the outside world and another on the inner. These are the travelers who can teach us about the human heart. Like Pico Iyer writes, they travel with open hearts and eyes to find themselves, 'to shake up our complacencies by seeing all the moral and political urgencies,

the life-and-death dilemmas, that we seldom have to face at home.' Marianne Peel is such a traveler; her sight, her heart, her pen bring us into a community of wise women and caring men scattered across the globe, in out-of-the-way places. Her book is a rich estuary, a houseboat of stories full of heart."
    —Jeremy Paden, author of *World As Sacred Burning Heart*

"From the beautiful to the unimaginable, compassion radiates from 'the underbelly of each word' of *No Distance Between Us* by Marianne Peel. The author's exquisite storytelling voice brings to life vivid characters with their human joys and heartbreaking struggles. The flavors and beauty of distant lands coexist with sickness, poverty, and tragedy. The poetry in this book opens our hearts 'to let in the light.' To hold each other's hands, and sing. And what brings me to tears the most is the life–changing personal journey of the speaker, the appreciation of each gesture, the generosity extended and received. Thank you, Marianne, for inviting us 'in your country.'"
    —Katerina Stoykova, author of *Second Skin*

No Distance Between Us

No Distance Between Us

a journey in poems

Marianne Peel

with foreword by Deni Naffziger

Shadelandhouse Modern Press
Lexington, Kentucky

A Shadelandhouse Modern Press book

No Distance Between Us
a journey in poems

For information about permission to reproduce selections from this book, please email permissions@smpbooks.com or direct written inquiries:
Permissions
Shadelandhouse Modern Press, LLC,
P.O. Box 910913, Lexington, KY 40591

Published in the United States of America by:

Shadelandhouse Modern Press, LLC
Lexington, Kentucky
smpbooks.com

First edition 2021

Shadelandhouse, Shadelandhouse Modern Press, and the colophon are trademarks of Shadelandhouse Modern Press, LLC.

Library of Congress Control Number: 2021946019
ISBN: 978-1-945049-20-0

Editor: Deni Naffziger
Book design and page layout: Brooke Lee
Cover design: Brooke Lee
Cover art: "Yearning to Roam," Jana Kappeler
Cover photo of starry sky: Will Stewart on Unsplash
Frontispiece: Alicia Kon
Illustrations: Annelisa Hermosilla
Lotus flower: Rattakan used with permission from Pixabay

for Sally McClintock, Murari Suvedi, Bill Richardson, and Patrick Mullan-Koufopoulos who celebrated and honored my desire to explore the world with an open and vibrant heart

Traveling—
it leaves you speechless,
then turns you into a storyteller.
—Ibn Battuta

Travel changes you. As you move through this life
and this world you change things slightly, you leave marks
behind, however small. And in return, life—and travel—
leaves marks on you. Most of the time, those marks—
on your body or on your heart—are beautiful.
Often, though, they hurt.

—Anthony Bourdain

No Distance Between Us

CONTENTS

Lesvos

Israel

Ukraine

Nepal

China

Close to Home

FOREWORD

This being human is a guest house.
Every morning a new arrival.

A joy, a depression, a meanness,
some momentary awareness comes
as an unexpected visitor.

Welcome and attend them all!
Even if they're a crowd of sorrows,
who violently sweep your house
empty of its furniture,
still, treat each guest honorably.
He may be clearing you out
for some new delight.

From "The Guest House"—Rumi, translated by Coleman Barks

MARIANNE PEEL's collection, *No Distance Between Us*, is filled with poems of discovery. Through her extensive travels, the narrator's revelations are often more internal than they are about any foreign geography or culture. Amazed, confused, perplexed, often frustrated, her interior journey is where the ultimate epiphanies lie. And, just as Rumi suggests, the key is in accepting and welcoming whatever lessons we glean along our way. This narrator's outward journey takes place over six regions, and while we are privy to her experiences, as readers we also bear witness to her emotional and spiritual transformation—the lessons she learns as the result of her expeditions.

No Distance Between Us opens in the northern Aegean Sea off the coast of Turkey. "Fear is the Sea That Carries Me" tells the story of a refugee, an outsider, who (like the narrator herself) dreams of finding comfort in a foreign land, perhaps with a "steaming cup of cardamom chai placed in our shivering hands." This man's experience is far more brutal than most of us will ever face; however, the final image reflects the comfort that all of us desire, whether traveling abroad or within our own sphere. The following poems in this first section, including "Lunch Break at Kara Tepe Refugee Camp" and "Ubuntu: The Clothing Store Queue at Kara Tepe Refugee Camp," provide additional reminders that our narrator is far from home, an outsider in what appears to be a merciless place. She realizes: "There are no olive trees for shade here, / just the blisters of full afternoon sun. / I take off my sandals, / feel the scorching pavement."

By the end of the first section, we find the narrator engaged in the work she traveled to do. In "The Man and His Words," she is teaching English, in an informal way, to a man who is eager to learn the language. He writes text on his hands, and she teaches him what the words mean—not only through neutral definitions but also by addressing more subtle meanings. At a certain point, she understands how deep language runs: "I knew there were so many words / already learned, embedded beneath the lines / on the palm of his hand."

But more importantly, by the last poem in the Lesvos section, both the narrator and the reader have settled in. The first leg of the journey begins with struggle and ends with the desire to hold a man's hand all night long, never speaking a word. The connotation is that they finally share the same language—no words necessary. And thus begins a cycle that Peel repeats in each section—the same cycle we all repeat when charting unfamiliar territory.

Next, we are swiftly uprooted to Israel and then to the Ukraine. We first land at a suicide bombing site in "The Collectors in Tel Aviv, Israel," where "... young men / with hard hats and yellow vests climb trees, / remove even the smallest branches / to capture minute pieces of flesh." There is little reflection in this poem. Rather, it is a documentation of horrors we can scarcely imagine. The day-to-day that these young men live can only be softened by the final image of the poem, a dream sequence that is prompted by a disembodied leg that one of the workers brings home: "The mute leg spent its night in the vestibule / propped against the hat rack. / In the bedroom upstairs, the couple dreamed / they were in a café, holding hands. / A clarinetist played Brahms Sonata No. 2 / while they drank cardamom coffee from fragile cups."

"Luba's Place" offers something different, something simultaneously familiar and strange. At the start of the poem, the narrator discloses that she knew Luba in an earlier time back in the United States. She remembers Luba crying over prepackaged slabs of meat at the grocery store, and we can't help but examine our own culture's insensitivity played out in the meat department. But now she is in Luba's Ukraine, a stranger squatting over a hole in the airport bathroom. "I am clumsy as I relieve myself, awkward / as I straddle this foreign place." She is the stranger here, taken by Luba's strength and apparent objectivity as she prepares supper. "That evening she kills a chicken for me. / I do not hear the bird howl as she breaks its neck." At the end of this section, we again take comfort in the narrator's satisfaction after dinner. She feels at home here: "Later that night there is a wedding in town, / and singing past four a.m. A tenor begins; / soon eight-part harmonies bellow into the night. / Lying in the dark, I hear their song. / Luba's chicken fills my satisfied stomach. / I no longer want for tea."

From there, the makeshift markets of Pokhara. "Bartering in Nepal" is a lovely poem of witness that immediately submerges the reader in a "day-in-the-life" experience and ends on a positive note when the narrator acknowledges that she has "received exactly the price I had bargained for." The poem, "Ashes," in the likeness of a poem by Arthur Sze, provides a more expansive historic and geographic perspective. It's a dark piece though a strong one. The Nepal section wraps up with "In the Courtyard," and, not coincidentally, "...the last day of my journey" in Nepal. It is a stunning poem of farewell with an awareness that: "We don't need light to hold one another, shadow to shadow, singing our way through the absence of light." And as any astute reader—any astute human being—knows, it's only through the darkness that we see light and, consequently, gain wisdom.

Then onto China with "Huangguoshu Waterfall," a poem of witness in which the narrator observes pointed differences between herself and the women of Guizhou who float across the rocks in high-heeled shoes, whereas she steps carefully (stellar metaphor) for fear that she will career off the rocks. "Seeking Sanctuary in Guiyang, China" begins: "In your country, my key does not fit the lock" (another strong metaphor—this collection is filled with them), and the reader is given a very detailed description of how she gains entry with the help of an old man. Maps are everywhere, but we soon discover (as our narrator does) that things aren't always as they appear. Even maps can't help her negotiate what is going on in her room. Again, the old man assists her, but later we see her become self-sufficient.

"In your country" also considers the narrator's differences. "I can't hear inflections, the ones you show me with your hands... ." By the end of that piece, the narrator remembers her students in Guiyang. They named her "bǎi líng niǎo," a songbird that sings through the fog, a skylark. This is, of course, a reminder that although she is an outsider, she is also a part of this tapestry. "Mahjong by Candlelight" is the delightful telling of a traditional Chinese game, which the narrator's students have been asking her to play for days. By the end of the poem, there is a switch: the teacher has become the student and the students her teachers! And together they "build yet another Great Wall of China." In "*Bing Pijiu*: Cold Beer," the narrator is finally comfortable enough that she confidently identifies the failings of her American teaching partner as the two of them drink and dine together at a local restaurant. Near the end of the poem, she proves to the discriminating chef that she can competently use chopsticks. "The Stone Poet Speaks to Me at the Ancient Weir Artist Village in Lishui" takes us deeper into that place a traveler has the good fortune to go—not just in terms of geographical placement, but in that deeper human connection to others, which she would not have experienced had she not ventured away from her homeland. And finally, the big picture is revealed in "Climbing Tiantai Mountain," when she ultimately feels her "rightful place in the family of all beings."

Eventually the traveler returns home, but there are journeys to be made here as well—physical, emotional, and spiritual. This last segment opens with "Lost and Found," a meditation on travel and intuition. It's followed by "Today You Are a River in My Hands"—another meditation on traveling: "Into rivers. / Into streams that would cross boundaries." The final poem, "We Are Peace," comes full circle as the narrator is grounded on home soil yet finds herself in an awkward situation with a Muslim man and his wife. As a reader, I understand in that moment she feels suddenly again like a foreigner "frozen in her own country, aware of the cultural divide." But as she has done throughout this transcendent collection, Marianne Peel brings the reader to an awareness that we must always continue to "reach across the divide."

Deni Naffziger
Author, *Desire to Stay*
Nominated for the 2015 Weatherford Award
Former editor, *Riverwind Literary Magazine*

LESVOS

Fear Is the Sea That Carries Me

Beat off the Turkish shore
by men with rigid batons, my body
bruised because they did not want me
here.

I am one sinking raft away
from safety. The smugglers
take our money, my wallet of photos,
my grandmother's engagement ring
which I wear on my finger.

My right eye is still swollen shut. My balance
crooked as I step onto the flimsy, overcrowded raft.

My father tells me of lights
on the rocky shore of Lesvos.
How residents from town—from Mytilene—
line their cars on flat places.

And so we steer our raft toward
makeshift lighthouses. Hoping
darkness will subside.
Hoping the night will not swallow us.

My father tells me they wait
for us with arms open. With blankets
they will drape around our shoulders.
A steaming cup of cardamom chai
placed in our shivering hands.

Lunch Break at Kara Tepe Refugee Camp

Walking down the steep hill to the grocery,
I see a man lean onto his daughter's elbow.

She balances him there, in that parking lot,
compensating for his missing leg.

They move methodically, always forward
closer to the electronic door.

I find the bin with spanakopita,
rummaging out the one with crusted edges.

I wish I craved olives, so many jars.
I settle for pomegranate juice and a brick of feta.

These I bury in my backpack
then hike to the loading dock for a sit.

There are no olive trees for shade here,
just the blisters of full afternoon sun.

I take off my sandals,
feel the scorching pavement.

My hands drip with olive oil,
flakes of phyllo dough.

Peacock anemones carpet the spring field.
Winged sea lavender blooms onto the rocky shore.

As I climb back up the hill,
I long for someone to kiss my pomegranate lips.

Ubuntu: The Clothing Store Queue at Kara Tepe Refugee Camp

Yesterday you crouched in the doorway
your fingers pushing the needle

in and out of cotton pants,
your tailor hands mending in the scorch of day.

Grandbaby asleep next to you,
one foot pumping on the edge

of the cradle, a silent lullaby.
Kitchen cat curled around your other ankle.

Today you wait in a queue of women,
your sandal broken at the bend.

I create a store ticket for you, a promise
of new shoes.

You hum and nod and touch my hair,
roll the ends through your fingers.

I ask the Farsi translator to tell you
how beautiful your face shimmers in the sun.

You take my face in your seamstress hands,
kiss one cheek and then the other.

I hold your shoulders in my hands,
hijab folding gently around my fingers.

A Gift from Zhino, the Kurdish Translator at Kara Tepe Refugee Camp

I
That morning an orange tabby darted
out of the shoe room, scrabbled
over my feet, exited the back of the tent
between refugees seeking shoes and clothing.
She cinched her babies at the scruff of their necks
teeth sunk in enough to secure the hold,
carried them out to the fields, behind the shop,
one by one.

By noon a nest of kittens in the long grasses.
There the song of mourning doves
lullabied her babies to sleep.

II
That morning I had no shoes to offer—
only flip flops for a man from Syria,
three sizes too big. Clownish
shoes, good for a laugh,
for a choreographed stunt.

I had no maternity underwear to offer
his wife, belly swelled beneath her burqa.
No hijab—the plastic bin was empty.
She longed for deep green, gold
thread, to frame her face,
to reveal the green flecks of light
in her eyes.

No football shoes for their daughter.
She showed me her left foot
was stronger than her right,
kicked an invisible ball
with one foot, then the other.

I had no socks for the baby. Toes cold
before morning sun warmed everything,
even the rocks at the roots of olive trees.

That morning I was bursting with *no*.
My mouth full of *I'm sorry*
and *this is all we have*
and *I wish I had more to give you*
and *I'm sorry your feet hurt*
from navigating rocks in the olive grove.
I could not stop from crying.

III
That morning, Zhino,
the Kurdish translator,
arrived with her mother.
She wanted to show me this matriarch
who had clutched the side of a raft
with all her strength and stamina
as they crossed the treacherous sea
between Turkey and Lesvos.

And later that morning
this woman would lie on a gurney
as a surgeon carved a tumor
from her brain.

IV
On that morning, Zhino asked
why mascara stained my cheeks,
why my eyes were red and swollen.
I told her about the many bare feet
I had held in the palms of my hands,
the many soles I could not protect
with shoes I did not have.

V
Zhino put her hand on the small of my back,
guided me to the back room, pointed
to a loose knit gray sweater on the floor
beneath the dishdashas, the men's Arabic robes.

"This is my crying place," she said.
"This is where I come to cry when I cannot stop
my crying. I will share my crying place
with you."

VI
That next morning
I found the kittens huddled in a nest
of grasses beside the olive tree.
Eyes open just a little, just enough
to let in the light.

The Man and His Words

I
I wanted to hold the hand
of the man who wrote English words
on his palm, that he might know
layers of meaning, the underbelly
of each word.

He waited for me
at the Kara Tepe Refugee Camp,
near the Chai House with "hello, salaam,"
a slight bend at the torso.

One day he opened his hand,
exposed the word: *curse.* I told him
a bad spell he might cast, how he might be tempted
to mumble swear words, to curse beneath his breath,
waiting in line for hours, for shoes
that are not broken.

One day he opened his hand,
revealed the word *sophisticated.*
I told him to imagine his sister
wearing a hijab that brings out the gold in her eyes,
that matches the glittering eye shadow reserved
for special at-home occasions. Shoes
with stiletto heels. An ankle bracelet. Fancy.
A sophisticated dresser.

He nodded, adding "like elegant,"
and I knew there were so many words
already learned, embedded beneath the lines
on the palm of his hand.

I wanted to hold the hand of the man
who wrote English words on his palm.
But the taboo of a woman touching
a Muslim man. Some say we are *loose,*
easily bedded, we Western women.

II
Yesterday, I held the man's foot in my hands
trying to fit him with a proper pair:
sandals, sneakers, clunky boots, penny loafers,
even a donated pair of burgundy wingtips,
but nothing fit. Nothing worked.

III
I wanted to hold his hand
all night long, soft and still.
Slowly, in the cradle of the night,
his words would bleed onto my palm
backwards, upside down.

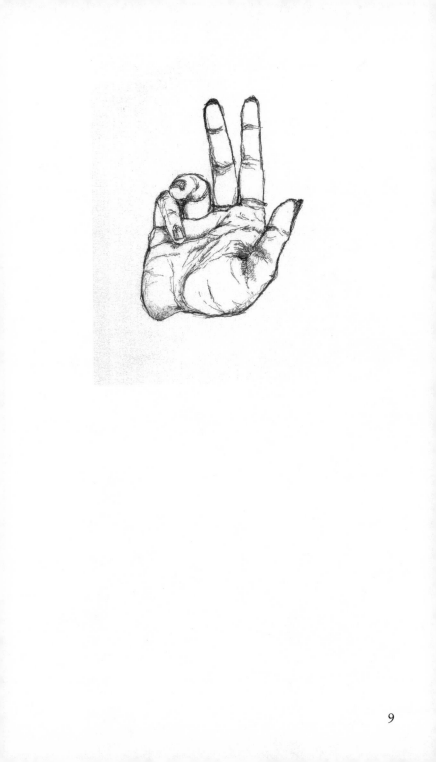

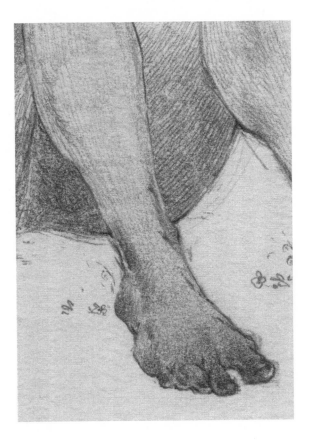

ISRAEL

The Collectors in Tel Aviv, Israel

At suicide bombing sites young men
with hard hats and yellow vests climb trees,
remove even the smallest branches
to capture minute pieces of flesh.

When their hands and arms cannot reach
body parts on rooftops or verandas
over the corner pizza parlor, they call in cranes
to fetch flesh from higher ground
to ensure an entire corpse is buried
within twenty-four hours,
as Jewish law requires.
Sometimes they use sponges to absorb
puddles of blood which they will squeeze
into pails and bury as the rabbi requires.
Remnant flesh and bone are placed in plastic
bags, separate receptacles for hands,
fingers, feet, and toes.

The bearded men are always on call,
even on the Sabbath.
They wait for word with walkie-talkies
dangling from their belts.
Their headquarters, nomadic—
underground bomb shelters
old fireworks storage areas
abandoned warehouses.
In these waiting places,
they chant the kaddish.
Prayer shawls from their bar mitzvahs
are draped over neon vests.

According to custom, the men must be married
to do this job, must be locked into other
steady employment. Psychologists believe
those who mate and work are the most stable,
the most emotionally secure. Though most
men leave this job after scavenging
the first ten sites, weary from ferreting,
and the diligent scraping.
They cannot seal and meticulously label
even one more bag.

Once a collector forgot to turn over
a leg to the authorities,
ended up taking the silent appendage
home to show his wife.
The mute leg spent its night in the vestibule
propped against the hat rack.

In the bedroom upstairs, the couple dreamed
they were in a café, holding hands.
A clarinetist played Brahms Sonata No. 2
while they drank cardamom coffee
from fragile cups.

UKRAINE

Luba's Place

I remember Luba crying
at a Michigan meat counter years ago
over pre-packaged slabs of pork and beef,
blood-red, obscenely thick.
Rare in her world.

Now, in Luba's Ukraine,
the airport bathroom offers only a hole
and two places to plant my feet.
I am clumsy as I relieve myself, awkward
as I straddle this foreign place.

At Luba's house, everything looks tired.
The washing machine decrepit, weary.
Even the pig is exhausted.
But the garden is alive, and she takes pride
in the lattice that anchors the vines to her garden gate.
Phlox meander lazily beneath a melancholy sky.

Luba lights the stove with newspaper,
tells stories of ancestors who covered their dead
with white lace. She has become an old woman—
a Ukrainian still life on a stoop in a babushka
who makes her own noodles, dries apples for compote,
simmers borscht with grated beet root in the wooden stove.

The knit slippers by her door could fit my feet.
But my calves are weak next to Luba's,
my hands shamefully smooth.
I just want a cup of tea.
But the black night is soot thick.

I'd have to go to the woodpile,
drag water from the well, and then heat it.

And I just can't. Tea is a luxury in this place.

That evening she kills a chicken for me.
I do not hear the bird howl as she breaks its neck.
Luba's movements are quick.

Later that night there is a wedding in town,
and singing past four a.m. A tenor begins;
soon eight-part harmonies bellow into the night.

Lying in the dark, I hear their song.
Luba's chicken fills my satisfied stomach.
I no longer want for tea.

NEPAL

Bartering in Nepal

Tibetan women line the streets of Pokhara,
without the advantage of owning a shopping stall.
They create makeshift markets that tumble from a duffel bag.
Tibetan women are determined.
They say "yes thank you" to my "no thank you."

There are vendors late into the evening, too,
pouring light on their wares with matches or cigarette lighters
so passersby may see.
One woman spreads a cloth on the stoop,
invites me to sit next to her.

I shoo flies from my feet and ankles.
She tells me she has no home,
that she is a refugee from Tibet
here in Nepal, to earn a living.
She is a woman without a country.

I watch the jewelry multiply.
Mandela necklaces, gemmed earrings,
chains of silver that sparkle in the noonday sun.
She unravels rolls and rolls of wares,
creates a showcase one foot from the gutter.

She does not ask where I am from
nor how long I will stay in Pokhara.
Instead, she shows me a candlestick.
"Unique," she says,
"like no other."

She turns its center with her fingers
until a lotus blossom flowers.
"In the center," she tells me, "you place a candle."
"Not like clothes or paper.
This you will use for your whole life."
We barter rupees.
I try to remember dollar equivalencies,
but fail to calculate as she opens and closes,
opens and closes the lotus blossom.

Just as the lotus is in full flower,
a man plants his trekking sandals on her cloth.
"Whatever she tells you, the price is one fourth,"
he warns in his British accent.
"Just yesterday she sold me a necklace for two thousand rupees.
I found the exact one down the street for five hundred.
She cheated me. She was dishonest,
and I'll be damned if I'll let her take advantage of you, too.
Be cautious. Be wary of this woman."
And he walks away,
leaves his footmark of dirt on her blanket.

I give her the rupees we had agreed upon,
our street-side contract, knowing
I have received exactly the price I had bargained for.

Ashes

"Opportunities come, but do not linger."
—Nepalese Proverb

This afternoon my friend wanders out to her California garden.
To gather abundance. To reap the harvest of her labors. Wildfires
blot out the sun on her slope of land. Shriveled vines laden
with soot. She returns to her barren kitchen with empty hands.
Her face is covered with ash.

And this afternoon, an ancient redwood burns near Big Basin.
Eighteen hundred years of growing. Fifty feet in circumference.
So many acres burned to ash. Nothing has escaped.
Tree roots suddenly mute.
Flames claw their way to dizzying limbs.

At 3 a.m. a biologist cannot sleep. Fire induced insomnia.
He watches the live webcam of a California condor nest.
A five-month-old chick still unable to fly.
Swallowed by flame.
The camera a blessing and a curse.

Once, in 2008, a condor chick found sanctuary
nesting in the tall redwoods. Far above the flames.
Survived the fire. Emerged covered with soot and ash.
The biologist named her *Phoenix*. Burn scars remain
on the redwoods that saved her.

And this afternoon, Nepalese boys climb
the sunrise mountains of Pokhara
with boulders strapped to their backs.
These young boys long to be British Gurkha soldiers.
To bring honor to their families. To be paid
more than a living wage.
Better to die than be a coward, their motto.

23

Hopefuls run uphill,
hauling wicker hod baskets on their backs.
Seventy pounds of weight on their bones.
Proof they are fierce, tough. Masculine.

If chosen, they carry the kukri into battle.
Traditional curved blade, eighteen inches long.
If the knife fails to draw blood in battle,
they must cut themselves. Blood bond.
Feeding a hungry weapon.

And these same young men haul buckets of soap
every evening to the river. They hawk van-washing talents
at the base of the mountain. Two buckets, four hands
slather a muddy vehicle into shine.
Rupees heavy in their pockets.

The water is filled with remnants from the temple.
Cremation ceremonies sing at the top
of the Annapurna range.
Ashes furl into the wind.
Sparks of life now burned to black
find their way to the water. Blend
with soap suds in the pails.

Washrags heavy,
soaked with the charred remains
of ancient ancestors.

Twelve Hours in Pokhara, Nepal

I   7 a.m.
You could not know.
You did not smell the jasmine
along the uneven centuries-old steps,
steps perplexing to symmetrical Western feet,
stumbling on rocks covered with moss and dew.

II   8 a.m.
You did not see her eyes,
blurred blue spots congealed over
the color of Nepalese morning tea,
oblivious to shadows shrouding the Annapurna.

> You did not see her hands,
> fists without fingers. No white linen bandages
> to conceal what leprosy stole.
> I wonder how she will hold the rupees tossed to her.

III   10 a.m.
You could not know.
You did not see her face,
this four-year-old with the sunrise at her back
perched on a stone wall
sucking her fingers.

> The cookie I place in her hand
> is filled with rich mango crème.
> She unscrews the wafer,
> the flavor of the fruit
> from the inside out.

IV   11 a.m.
You did not hear her voice
descending the steps of the Hindu temple.
The bell ringing after dyed red rice
is pressed into her forehead, homage to the Monkey God.

> She slips her hand in mine,
> balancing me in this crooked place
> singing *Sha la la la la*
> in the morning
> *Sha la la la la* in the evening.

> I respond *My lord, what a morning*
> and *When I fall on my knees with my face to the rising sun.*
> We weave a symphony of morning songs
> patchwork gifts of honor and blessing
> to the light of this day and all days.

V   5 p.m.
You could not know.
You did not see his hands,
orchestrating folk songs,
the blind truly leading the blind.
His vision is partial, he tells me.

> He sees shadows, some color.
> He moves among the sightless singers,
> mingles with the flute and bellows player,
> cueing them with the rhythm of his body.

> His arms conduct largo, then vivace,
> transforming the tempo of the melody.
> His hands convey nuance,
> conducting blind musicians
> unburdened with sheet music.

In this courtyard,
they celebrate the Tihar festival
for a plate of rupees and rice,
a picnic feast of sweet and savory
consumed late at night.

You did not feel his hands
tight around my own
accepting the invitation
to join the dance.

We are synchronized in our swaying.
I follow his lead, dance to "Resham Phiriree."
"There is no distance between us," he tells me.
"I will always think of you with love and remembrance."
He is blind to my face and my eyes that cannot keep from singing.
We hold hands, silent and still,
many measures after the music ceases.

In the Courtyard

On the last day of my journey, I sat by a river
of long, tangled hair. I rented a foot-paddle boat,
decorated our craft with Nepalese prayer flags,
homemade candles made of Coca–Cola bottles
and packed sand, added tapers from Pokhara marketplace.
I set sail, embellished with light and flags.

Yesterday I watched the children play in the water.
They drank dark liquid from Coke bottles bobbing
around a compliant water buffalo. Everyone coexisted
in the river. So much laughter bubbled up and around.

There is no ash here from the crematorium at the top
of the mountain. No smell of plastic burning on hillsides
or underpasses like in Kathmandu. Just the river
and the Annapurna range. A place of water and stone.

I could not say farewell to the children
at the Blind School. But Lakshmi took my hand,
led me to the playground outside the open-air
cinder block classroom. A place where chalk
was a rare commodity.

Lakshmi sat me down
on the cement around the olive tree.
Her eyes blurred at their center.
Gold flecks of fireworks exploded from the edges.
Lakshmi can still see shadows.
She wrapped a blanket around my shoulders,
touched my arms with tenderness and began to sing.
The playground transformed into a tableau.
Everything suddenly still.
Even the birds grew quiet as Lakshmi sang
"My Heart Will Go On."

Her song—a farewell with a promise. To remember
this place where children from all over Nepal come
to wait for increasing shadows, where they shepherd
each other into darkness.

Lakshmi held my hands as she sang.
We don't need light to see.
We don't need light to hold one another,
shadow to shadow, singing our way
through the absence of light.

CHINA

Huangguoshu Waterfall

I am behind this water, beneath
this waterfall in a remote Chinese village.
Here in Guizhou Province local women come
to these rocks and falling waters with stiletto heels,
embroidered lacy umbrellas, Ruby Woo lipstick.

I step carefully, fearing my rubber-soled sandals
will fail me. That I will career off the rocks. I am
a plummet of clear plastic poncho and sunflower seeds
sold in clear zippered bags, sold by children bartering
in crevices along the climb.

But the women of Guizhou float across the rocks,
their high-heeled shoes hydroplane them across the waters.
Their umbrellas lift them skyward, these umbrellas designed
only for sunshade. Out of their red mouths, a familiar folk melody.
"Jasmine Flower." Unison singing. A fluid choir of treble voices.

These women are a procession of elegant sculptures. A soundtrack
of pentatonic scales. Notes reverberating in earth, wood,
metal, fire, and water. Voices flowing from a liquid score.

Seeking Sanctuary in Guiyang, China

In your country, my key does not fit the lock.
No amount of twisting and turning will turn it over.
An old man offers cooking oil
to unhinge the lock, to help me enter
an old Peace Corps apartment.

He pours oil into the keyhole, slowly
greases the inner workings. He holds my hand,
guides the key through a sea of oil
until the door clicks open.

Maps are everywhere, floor to ceiling studded
with multicolored push pins marking places
others have lived. The walls are speckled
with small black dots; the wallpaper
appears to float. I turn to thank him.

When I open my mouth to say *"xie xie,"*
black dots fly into my mouth.
Frenzied mosquitoes swarm
between my lips. The old man holds my chin firm
with his thumb, clears my palate as his index finger
gouges insects from my mouth.

Later at the market,
I buy plastic for the windows,
netting for my bed.
I zip myself in,
listen to mosquitoes bang against the windows.

Outside machines run all night long,
construction crews work beneath electric lamps,
breaking concrete in the moonlight.

In your country

I can't hear inflections,
the ones you show me with your hands
directing a symphony of words
scooping air, song rising from your palms.

Your Mandarin sings with quarter tones
as I sit on my haunches in Monkey Park
listening for the line, the arc,
the story your words tell with your hands.
Your gestures—like songbirds at daybreak
that congregate along the gate,
leap into brittle air, no masks
to save them from coal ash.
I wonder if the dust will choke their song.

The first time I was in Guiyang,
my students named me *bǎi líng niǎo*:
a songbird that sings through the fog,
a skylark carrying melody
like breadcrumbs or seeds
between the hinges of a broken beak.

Mahjong by Candlelight

They've been asking me for days
to play mahjong,
often enjoyed with beer, spirits, smoking,
and money passed from fist to fist.
They escort me to the dormitory six flights up.
We rattle out our umbrellas into the hall.

The entire floor of men has arrived,
gathered to watch a foreign woman stumble
her way through the intricacies
of stacked bricks. They tell me to create
the Great Wall of China, the game a disguise
to scry out secrets.
They want my advice
hoping my Western ways will illuminate their path.

The men wash their feet in the bucket on the balcony,
take their places around the tiles.
They huddle and whisper their experience
into my ears, advising
which brick to keep,
which to throw away.
Nudging the proper move,
the most advantageous strategy.

Our faces are closer, our foreheads
nearly touching, in this crowded mahjong place.
This place mutely absent from the Lonely Planet guidebook.
I realize I am far from where most westerners
are willing to walk and work.
We have traveled kilometers from the classroom.

We reverse roles, exchange our familiar places.
They become my patient mentors.

The lightning flexes across the sky.
We are crackled into darkness by the collision of heat and light.
My teachers light the bricks with cell phone illumination.
"A romantic game with the candles, yes?" Jiang Xue asks.
He runs to the store for luminaries. On his return,
we build yet another Great Wall of China.

Bing Pijiu: Cold Beer

My American teaching partner wanted her beer
cold. She suggested a bucket of ice,
demanded it,
noontime after noontime.
She refused to learn Mandarin,
preferred shouting "cold beer"
louder and louder, insisting
the cook comply.

That morning I snuck into the kitchen,
watched the chef slice chicken necks
and onions on an old tree stump.
Every cut embedded in the rings.
He was quick with the knife—
my head dizzy with each spark of the blade.

I pointed to the case of beer in the corner,
mimed a shiver, whispered
the Mandarin words I knew,
"*bing pijiu,*" cold beer.
I knew he had no ice.

At noon, he arrived with beer,
tightly wrapped in a cold, wet towel.
She did not thank him.
No *xie xie* for this innovative chef.
"Not cold enough," she told me.
"Not nearly cold enough."

He handed me a bowl of noodles,
the "la," the spice, fragmented red,
pigmenting the broth.
For me he added bok choy, spinach,
and a fried egg, the yolk a runny yellow-orange.
Beneath the egg: five peanuts.
A rare gift in this place of monk meals.

I took my chopsticks in hand, showed him
how this Western woman could pluck
a single peanut. He nodded, smiled,
returned to the kitchen stump,
raised the blade for our dinner—
to the neck of one more chicken.

The Stone Poet Speaks to Me at the Ancient Weir Artist Village in Lishui

You did not see the fog settle in the bamboo grove
merging with my breath, my breathing.
Cold and determined clouds,
air fusing with air.

You did not smell the sizzle of dumplings,
the plate of pickled vegetables.
Red peppers and chilies she offered me on a wooden spoon.
Fire adhered to my lips, a sunrise burning the gray morning.

You did not hear the lady of the lake
murmuring a morning song as she soothed
and rubbed her face, shoulders,
the bob of her breasts,
hair released from clasps, free of braids.

You did not see the potter by the river
hands shaping clay, seducing
curves and indentations with thumb and forefinger.
He is alone by the river, breathing mist
onto the glazed vessel in his hands.

You did not see the jagged edge
where the stone poet raised his arm,
silently urging me to huddle in the cove of his chest,
there, down by the waters.

"Listen to the rhythm here,
buried deep beneath skin and muscle and sinew.
Listen down to the marrow place."
He tells me, "I cannot sleep, ever.
This pulsing keeps me awake."

He takes my hand, eases it gently behind the threads of his gown
into the warm liquid surrounding the beating.
"Take my heart in your hands. Massage it softly,
with steady rhythm. So that I may sleep."

And so in the fog of the bamboo grove,
I hold this poet's beating heart,
watch his eyes close,
tranquil in the fog.

Climbing Tiantai Mountain

The Chinese believe that showing all at once,
revealing all in a swoop of sensation,
is simply obscene.

Instead, breath by breath,
a new sight at each curve, each turn.
Always more to reveal.

One rung
from the top of the mountain,
there is incense.

I feel it curl around my face,
beneath my fingernails,
into the pores of my mountain-climbing skin.

I have ascended to the temple,
knowing the top of a mountain
is the only soulful place for worship.

An intermittent gong.
Apples and peaches on the offering table.
Flowers along the path.

A phoenix carved into the sky
coexists with the dragon.
There is no yearning here, no hesitancy.

Just the permeating incense
and feeling my rightful place
in the family of all beings.

CLOSE TO HOME

Lost and Found

She lacked certain aptitudes
when traveling. Her children define her
as geographically challenged. Perpetually lost.

For her, directionality comes with landmarks.
Old Santiago's Fruit Market on the outskirts of town.
Ruth's General Store, intersection of Lester and Vine.

There is no north, south, east, or west. Except
when the singing bowl sings, when she is called
to face each direction. To honor the lessons of her ancestors.

To the East, a rising yellow tide
of sun and sacred tobacco. Eagle covers the sky
between birch and poplar.

To the North, a winter afghan of ivory. Wind
and wisdom of the elders. Bear scratches his back,
soothes the aching itch on the bark of a cedar tree.

To the South, the black muck land of earth, sweet
grass barely protruding. Wolf lingers
at the base of the oak.

To the West, burgundy autumn. Moving
waters. The full-throated dream of the Buffalo,
shapeshifting.

Healing in all directions. Abundance and the receiving
of chi. Gift of solid ground. Here she intuits
her way. Here she is never lost.

Today You Are a River in My Hands

Every morning I wonder if the anhinga will appear
on the bow of our boat. A piano in flight, this bird.
White and black feather keys pressed against
a February sky. She resonates a harpsichord tune.
Scales her flight to the post on the Banana River.
At dusk she plays a divertimento. At sunset, a sonata.
She serenades a fisherwoman on the dock
as she hooks shrimp onto her line. Today
I sing your body into oceans. Into rivers.
Into streams that would cross boundaries.
I fashion you into a tributary. An estuary.
Swirl the brine of your waters with the fresh of mine.
Flow into my chanting streams. Let us be lovers
and live on these waters. Houseboat brimming with books.

Saturday Night at the Symphony

She used to sit on the fire escape Saturday nights,
waiting for the symphony to begin.

Couldn't afford a real ticket. Not even
to a Sunday matinee.

Cheap seats. Standing room only.
Nosebleed section.

She didn't mind the rust
on the fire escape, the way it left

a waffle pattern on her backside,
on the soft underneath of her thighs.

I marked my calendar. Deliberately
walked her alley every Saturday night.

Watched her close her eyes as the overture began.
The way she leaned her head on the railing.

Wished I'd brought her a pillow or a cup of hot cocoa
or a plaid shawl to wrap around her shoulders.

I watched her conduct. First
with one hand, then both.

She cued in the trombones. Extended
her right hand to the tipping point of the slide.

When the cello section played, she put both hands
to her throat, as if she couldn't breathe.

Allowed an exhale only when the strings
finished on a Picardy third.

She swayed forward and back as the bassoon played.
Executed a slow chromatic scale.

Eighth note by eighth note until
it landed at the valley of its range.

When the piccolo played, she jumped from step to step,
matched her feet to the first of a quartet of sixteenth notes.

She arabesqued her way up the fire escape, took flight
among stars pulsing to the rhythm of her improvisation.

Confession

I'm going to miss the trees
the most, you tell me. On the sand,
in our anti-gravity chairs. We float
toward and away from each other.
You've let your hair grow gray, working
its way from root to shoulders.

Last year you turned fifty. Cleaned out
your closet. Donated everything. Including
your red-soled stilettos. Purged anything
sensual. Off the shoulder sweaters. Spandex
skirts. Anything that snugged the curves.

You have runner's legs. Marathons. Stamina
for the distance, but still envy
the muscles in my calves. Dancer's legs.
I tell you I once performed forty-two relevés
on point shoes. Won the competition at the studio.
Nothing is as it seems beneath the tulle

and the sequined bodice. I chose to pad my toes
with lambswool. Rejected the synthetic pad. Wanted
nothing manufactured or artificial. Wanted to feel the softness
on my toes as I manipulated them into steel-toed
shoes two sizes too small. Soft pink ribbons
up the ankles. After the barre work, after the floorwork,

after forty-two relevés, the lambswool
was crusted with blood. Sacrificial lamb.
Lamb for slaughter. You tell me you lost
one toenail at a time in Greece. Running

the same marathon path naked boys ran
generations ago.

You look out onto an alley. Bougainvillea
emerging from cracks in the rocks. From cracks
in the bricks. There is a name for the emergence
of stems and flowers and vines from stone.
But you have forgotten it.

A mustached man serenaded you
with a klezmer tune on his clarinet.
Lured you into his restaurant with a song.
You shared the same cigarette. Fire passed
between you. He promised to meet you
at the finish line. With an Efes beer from Turkey,
a lit cigarette. Today, you tell me
you will miss the trees most.

You imagine yourself erased. Just gone.
You are a shroud of open weave, mesh, and light.
Sitting in a wicker rocker. Listening to your daughter
play *Moonlight Sonata.* Beethoven on an autumn
afternoon. You imagine Beethoven sawing the legs
off his piano. Hearing the vibrations through floorboards.

We Are Peace

At first the peace rally on Grand River Avenue
is a riot of horns, wild honking, exuberant waving
from car windows. A man leans out from a store front,
flashes two thumbs up for the signs we hold:
Welcome Muslim Refugees and Immigrants.

A car screams by—its driver shouts, "Muslims go home!"
Another shakes his head, yells, "Yeah, until one of them kills
someone you love."

Then you stop your car to talk to me, record the ragtag
collection of activists with your cell phone.
You take pictures of signs that advocate love over fear,
compassion over hatred, acceptance over rejection,
trust over suspicion.

I am moved to step from the median, down the curb
to the driver's side window and reach out
to touch your hand when you stop me.
"I am a Muslim man. I cannot shake your hand."

In that moment, I am entirely aware of my femaleness,
frozen in my own country, aware of the cultural divide.
Beside him, his female companion.
"She can touch you," he assures me.
"She can hold your hand."

So, I reach across the divide.
We stop traffic with a single touch.

Acknowledgements

I AM grateful to the editors of the following publications in which some of the poems in this book, sometimes in earlier versions, first appeared.

Coming of Age: Writing & Art by Kentucky Women Over 60 (Red Lick Valley Press): "Fear Is the Sea That Carries Me"

Common Chord Anthology (Universal Table/Wising Up Press): "We Are Peace"

Defenestrationisonism.net: "A Gift from Zhino, the Kurdish Translator at Kara Tepe Refugee Camp"

Evansville Review: "The Man and His Words"

Kentucky Philological Review: "Lunch Break at Kara Tepe Refugee Camp"

Kosmos Quarterly: "Today You Are a River in My Hands"

Naugatuck River Review: "A Gift from Zhino, the Kurdish Translator at Kara Tepe Refugee Camp"

Quartet Journal: "Confession"

Young Ravens Literary Review: "Climbing Tiantai Mountain"

A Note of Gratitude

IT TAKES a village to provide safe sanctuary for a writer. I have been blessed with numerous mentors. I'd like to thank Judy Volk and Donna Greeves, my high school and junior high school English teachers, respectively, who first taught me to trust my voice. My Poetry Mama, Joyce Benvenuto, always takes time to comment directly on my poems and sends them to me, old school, through snail mail, for decades. Being a forever student, I'd like to thank the poetry teachers in my life who have encouraged me to write without fear: Katerina Stroykova, Julie Maloney, Jan Freeman, Anita Skeen, Leila Chatti, Laura Apol, Libby Falk Jones, Deni Naffziger Hackworth, Rick Horst, Janine Certo, Sherine Gilmour, Wilderness Sarchild, Wendy DeGroat, and Marge Piercy.

A special thanks to my Mindfulness Full Moon Drumming group: Joan Denton, Lisa Meadows, Susan Crosswait, Glennes Drennan, and Brenda Todd. My gratitude to the poets in the Coming-of-Age Project, Berea, Kentucky: Marta Dorton, Kathleen Gregg, Shelda Hale, and Catherine Perkins. My gratitude for the people in my life who read and respond to my poems in so many helpful and authentic ways: Therese Dawe Wood, Daphne Mitchell, Patricia Frank, Ellen Hoard, Mary Anna Kruch, Ed Middleton, Mary Zimmerman, Jack Johnson, Diana Hrabowecki, Marie Kuzych, Sandy Maxim, Carol Schwartz, Hope Nichols Smith, Mary Cinnamon, Beth Mundy, Kara Foster, Hilary Lowbridge, Donna Kaplowitz, Liz Denny, LeTonia Jones, Marika Lindholm, Martin Willits Jr, and Peyton Adams. Thanks to Virginia H. Underwood, publisher, Shadelandhouse Modern Press, for reaching out and believing in me.

Special thanks to my daughters—Alicia, Audrey, Annelise, and Allegra—who taught me to listen with a poet's ear and heart, as they spoke poems on car rides, all the time. And finally, infinite gratitude to my partner Scott Vander Ploeg, my beloved, as we sit across from each other writing, playing with words, together.

About the Author

MARIANNE PEEL is a poet, actor, musician, and retired English teacher. She served as a public-school educator for 32 years and continues to engage in field instructor work with various universities, supervising education interns in the classroom. She spent three summers in Guizhou Province, teaching best practices to teachers in China, and has received Fulbright-Hays Program awards to further her research in Nepal (2003) and Turkey (2009) and to support her work as a teacher.

Peel's poetry awards include the Alpine Fellowship Writing Prize (2021, longlisted); Wheelbarrow Books Poetry Prize at Michigan State University (finalist); the Naugatuck River Review Annual Narrative Poetry Contest (2020, finalist), the Jelly Bucket literary journal Poetry Prize and Genre Prize; and the ESME (Empowering Solo Moms Everywhere) social platform's first place in poetry. She was awarded a summer residency at Eastern Kentucky University (2017) and participated in Marge Piercy's juried Intensive Poetry Workshop (2016), as well as Anita Skeen's Narrative Poetry Workshop at Georgia O'Keefe's Ghost Ranch in New Mexico.

Peel's poems have been published in several online and print literary journals. Her poem "Fear Is the Sea That Carries Me" was published in *Coming of Age: Writing & Art by Kentucky Women over 60*, co-edited by Libby Falk Jones and Julianne Unsel. Peel's poem "Notes to My Autistic Daughter," was published in the collaborative debut anthology *We Got This: Solo Mom Stories of Grit, Heart and Humor*, co-edited by Marika Lindholm, Cheryl Dumesnil, and Katherine Shonk, which received a prestigious starred review by *Kirkus Reviews* and garnered several independent book awards. *No Distance Between Us* is Peel's debut book.